GW00601813

A
FEAST OF EASY CAROLS

ARRANGED FOR
PIANO BY

CAROL BARRATT

ILLUSTRATED
BY

WENDY HOILE

CHESTER MUSIC

THE★FIRST★NOWELL

English Carol

The— first——— Now——ell, the— An — gel did say, Was to

cer — tain poor shep – herds in fields as they lay; In— fields——— where—

they lay— keep—ing their sheep, On a cold win—ter's night— that

CHORUS

was — so deep. Now—ell,— Now—ell, Now—ell, Now —

-ell, Born is the King— of Is ———— ra—el.

2. They lookèd up and saw a Star
   Shining in the East, beyond them far,
   And to the earth it gave great light,
   And so it continued both day and night.
           Nowell, Nowell . . .

3. And by the light of that same Star
   Three Wise Men came from country far;
   To seek for a King was their intent,
   And to follow the Star wherever it went.
           Nowell, Nowell . . .

4. This Star drew nigh to the north-west,
   O'er Bethlehem it took its rest,
   And there it did both stop and stay,
   Right over the place where Jesus lay.
           Nowell, Nowell . . .

5. Then entered in those Wise Men three,
   Full reverently upon their knee,
   And offered there, in His Presence,
   Their gold, and myrrh, and frankincense.
           Nowell, Nowell . . .

6. Then let us all with one accord
   Sing praises to our Heavenly Lord,
   That hath made Heaven and earth of nought,
   And with His Blood mankind hath bought.
           Nowell, Nowell . . .

COVENTRY ★ CAROL

English Carol

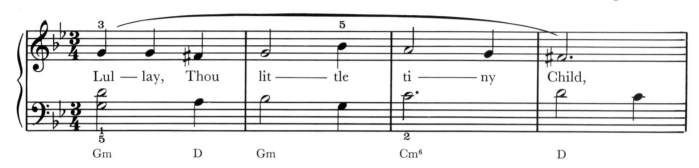

Lul — lay, Thou lit — tle ti — ny Child,

Gm   D   Gm   Cm⁶   D

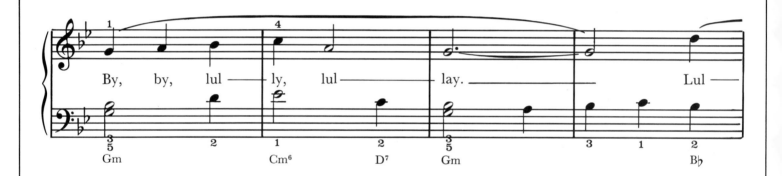

By, by, lul — ly, lul — lay.   Lul —

Gm   Cm⁶   D⁷   Gm   B♮

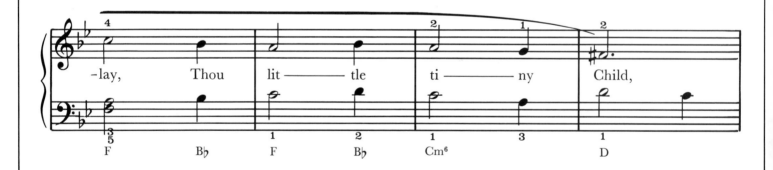

-lay, Thou lit — tle ti — ny Child,

F   B♮   F   B♮   Cm⁶   D

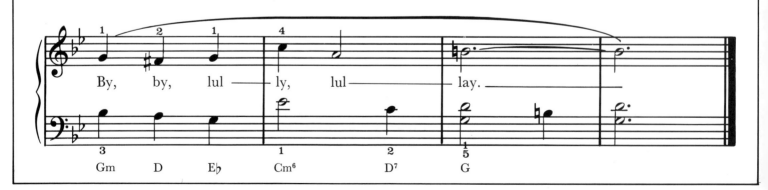

By, by, lul — ly, lul — lay.

Gm   D   E♭   Cm⁶   D⁷   G

2. Oh sisters, too, how may we do,
   For to preserve this day,
   This poor Youngling for whom we sing,
   By, by, lully, lullay.

3. Herod the King in his raging,
   Chargèd he hath this day
   His men of might, in his own sight,
   All children young to slay.

4. Then woe is me, poor child, for Thee,
   And ever mourn and say,
   For Thy parting nor say, nor sing,
   By, by, lully, lullay.

GLOUCESTERSHIRE ★ WASSAIL

English Carol

Was — sail, was — sail,___ all o — ver the town! ___ Our

bread it is white, and our ale___ it___ is brown, Our

bowl___ it___ is___ made of the white ma — ple tree; With the

was ——— sail — ing bowl we'll drink_____ to thee.

2. And here is to Dobbin* and to his right eye,
   Pray God send our master a good Christmas pie,
   And a good Christmas pie that we may all see;
   With our wassailing bowl we'll drink to thee.

3. And here is to Fillpail* and to her left ear,
   Pray God send our master a happy New Year,
   And a happy New Year as e'er he did see;
   With our wassailing bowl we'll drink to thee.

4. Come, butler, come fill us a bowl of your best,
   Then we hope your soul in Heaven may rest;
   But if you do bring us a bowl of the small,
   Then down shall go butler, bowl and all.

5. Then here's to the maid in the lily white smock,
   Who tripped to the door and slipped back the lock,
   Who tripped to the door and pulled back the pin,
   For to let us jolly wassailers in.

*Dobbin is a horse and Fillpail is a cow.

WENDY HOILE

Away·in·a·Manger

English Tune

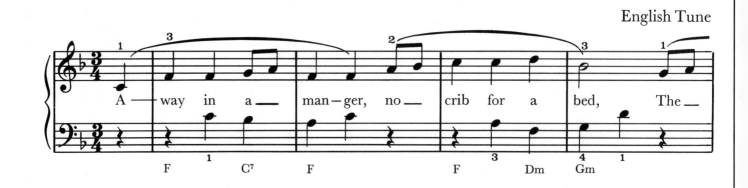

A — way in a — man — ger, no — crib for a bed, The —

F   C⁷   F   F   Dm   Gm

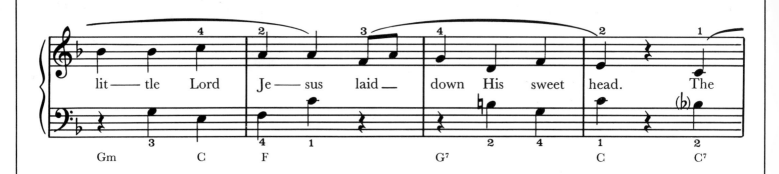

lit — tle Lord Je — sus laid — down His sweet head. The

Gm   C   F   G⁷   C   C⁷

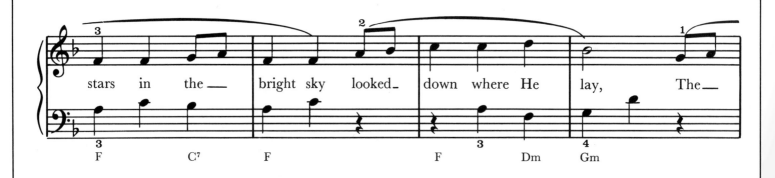

stars in the — bright sky looked — down where He lay, The —

F   C⁷   F   F   Dm   Gm

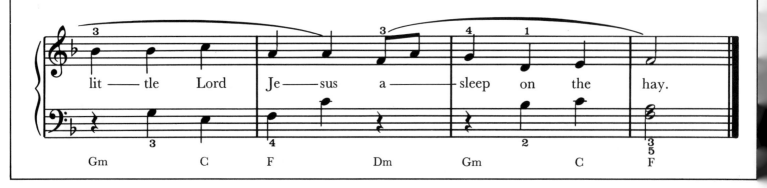

lit — tle Lord Je — sus a — sleep on the hay.

Gm   C   F   Dm   Gm   C   F

2. The cattle are lowing, the Baby awakes,
   But little Lord Jesus no crying He makes.
   I love Thee, Lord Jesus, look down from the sky,
   And stay by my side until morning is nigh.

3. Be near me, Lord Jesus, I ask Thee to stay
   Close by me for ever, and love me, I pray:
   Bless all the dear children in Thy tender care,
   And fit us for Heaven, to live with Thee there.

American Tune

GOD★REST★YOU★MERRY,★GENTLEMEN

English Carol

God rest you mer — ry, gen — tle — men, Let noth — ing you dis — may, Re — mem — ber Christ our Sa — viour Was born on Christ — mas day, To save us all from Sa — tan's power When we were gone a — stray.

CHORUS

O — ti — dings of com — fort and joy, com-fort and joy, O — ti — dings of com — fort and joy.

2. In Bethlehem, in Jewry,
   This blessèd Babe was born,
   And laid within a manger,
   Upon this blessèd morn;
   The which His mother Mary
   Did nothing take in scorn.
         O tidings . . .

3. From God our Heavenly Father
   A blessèd Angel came;
   And unto certain shepherds
   Brought tidings of the same:
   How that in Bethlehem was born
   The Son of God by name.
         O tidings . . .

4. "Fear not", then said the Angel,
   "Let nothing you affright,
   This day is born a Saviour
   Of a pure Virgin bright,
   To free all those that trust in Him
   From Satan's power and might".
         O tidings . . .

5. The shepherds at those tidings
   Rejoicèd much in mind,
   And left their flock a-feeding,
   In tempest, storm, and wind:
   And went to Bethlehem straightway,
   The Son of God to find.
         O tidings . . .

6. And when they came to Bethlehem
   Where our dear Saviour lay,
   They found Him in a manger,
   Where oxen feed on hay;
   His mother Mary kneeling down,
   Unto the Lord did pray.
         O tidings . . .

7. Now to the Lord sing praises,
   All you within this place,
   And with true love and brotherhood
   Each other now embrace;
   This holy tide of Christmas
   All others doth deface.
         O tidings . . .

ROCKING

Czech Carol

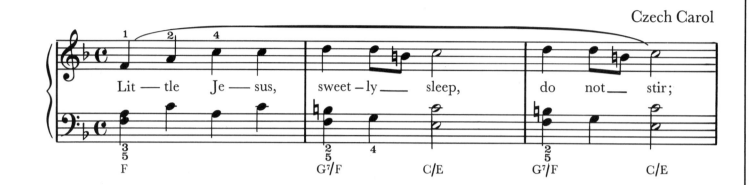

Lit — tle Je — sus, sweet – ly ___ sleep, do not ___ stir;

F   G⁷/F   C/E   G⁷/F   C/E

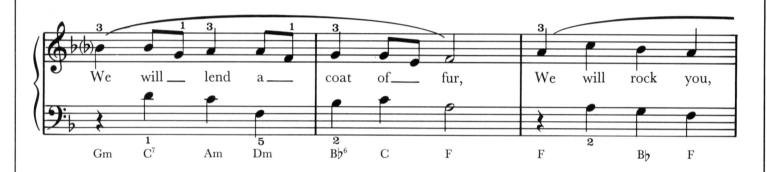

We will ___ lend a ___ coat of ___ fur, We will rock you,

Gm   C⁷   Am   Dm   B♭⁶   C   F   F   B♭   F

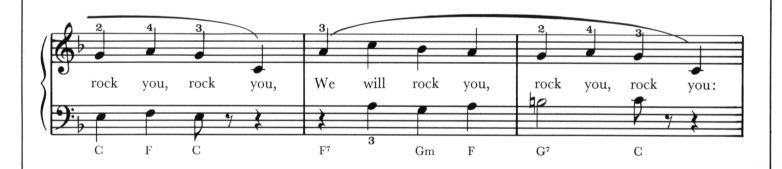

rock you, rock you, We will rock you, rock you, rock you:

C   F   C   F⁷   Gm   F   G⁷   C

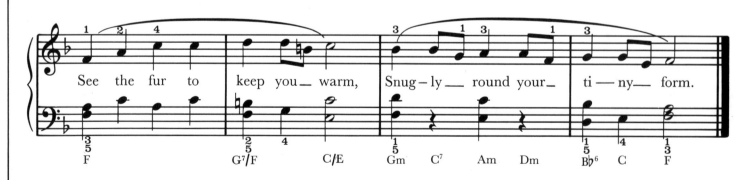

See the fur to keep you ___ warm, Snug – ly ___ round your ___ ti — ny ___ form.

F   G⁷/F   C/E   Gm   C⁷   Am   Dm   B♭⁶   C   F

Collected by Martin Shaw. The words were translated by Percy Dearmer.
From the Oxford Book of Carols, by permission of Oxford University Press

2. Mary's little baby, sleep, sweetly sleep,
   Sleep in comfort, slumber deep;
   We will rock you, rock you, rock you,
   We will rock you, rock you, rock you:
   We will serve you all we can,
   Darling, darling little man.

WE★THREE★KINGS

American Carol

We three Kings of O — ri — ent are,
Em   Em   B⁷   Em

Bear — ing gifts we tra — verse a — far,   Field and
Em   Em   B⁷   Em   Em

foun — tain, moor and moun — tain, Fol — low — ing yon — der
D   G   G   Am   Em   B⁷

CHORUS

star.   O, _____ Star of won — der, star of
Em   D⁷   G   G   C

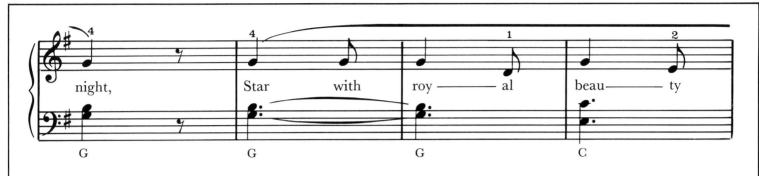

night, Star with roy — al beau — ty

G   G   G   C

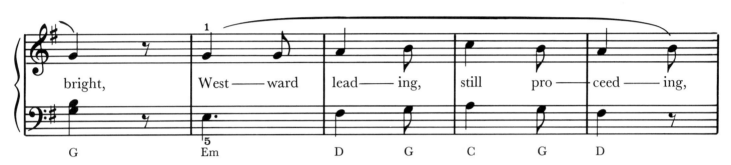

bright, West — ward lead — ing, still pro — ceed — ing,

G   Em   D   G   C   G   D

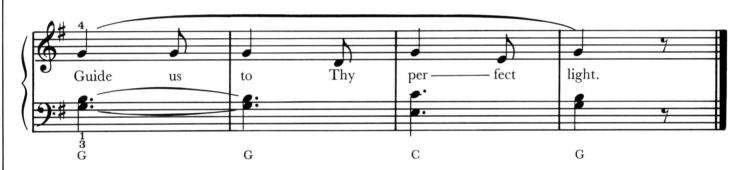

Guide us to Thy per — fect light.

G   G   C   G

2. *(Melchior)*
Born a King on Bethlehem plain,
Gold I bring to crown Him again,
King for ever, ceasing never,
Over us all to reign:
      O, Star of wonder . . .

4. *(Balthazar)*
Myrrh is mine; its bitter perfume
Breathes a life of gathering gloom;
Sorrowing, sighing, bleeding, dying,
Sealed in the stone-cold tomb:
      O, Star of wonder . . .

3. *(Caspar)*
Frankincense to offer have I;
Incense owns a Deity nigh;
Prayer and praising, all men raising,
Worship Him, God most high:
      O, Star of wonder . . .

5. *(All)*
Glorious now, behold Him arise,
King, and God, and sacrifice;
Heav'n sings Alleluia,
Alleluia the earth replies:
      O, Star of wonder . . .

WHILE★SHEPHERDS★WATCHED

WENDY HOILE

English Tune

While shep — herds watched their flocks by night, All seat — ed on the

F   C   Dm   Bb   F   C   F   Am   Gsus   G

ground, The An — gel of the Lord came down, And glo — ry shone a — round.

C   F   Bb   F   Gm   C   F   C   Dm Bb   C   F

16

2. "Fear not", said he; for mighty dread
   Had seized their troubled mind;
   "Glad tidings of great joy I bring
   To you and all mankind."

3. "To you in David's town this day
   Is born of David's line
   A Saviour, who is Christ the Lord;
   And this shall be the sign:"

4. "The heavenly Babe you there shall find
   To human view displayed,
   All meanly wrapped in swathing bands,
   And in a manger laid."

5. Thus spake the seraph; and forthwith
   Appeared a shining throng
   Of Angels praising God, who thus
   Addressed their joyful song:

6. "All glory be to God on high,
   And to the earth be peace;
   Good-will henceforth from Heaven to men
   Begin and never cease."

Alternative tune arranged from George F. Handel

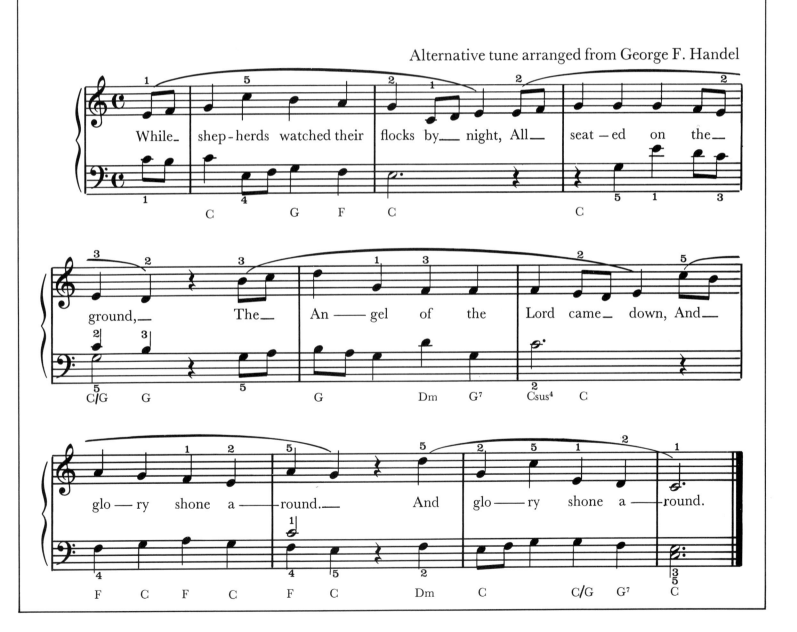

SEE ★ AMID ★ THE ★ WINTER'S ★ SNOW

English Carol

See a-mid the win—ter's snow, Born for us on earth be-low,

See, the ten—der Lamb ap—pears, Pro—mised from e——ter——nal years.

CHORUS

Hail, thou e—ver bles—sed morn. Hail, re-demp-tion's hap—py dawn.

Sing through all Je—ru——sa—lem, Christ is born in Beth—le—hem.

2. Lo, within a manger lies
   He who built the starry skies;
   He, who throned in height sublime,
   Sits amid the Cherubim.
           Hail, thou ever blessed . . .

3. Say, ye holy shepherds, say,
   What your joyful news today;
   Wherefore have ye left your sheep,
   On the lonely mountain steep?
           Hail, thou ever blessed . . .

4. "As we watched at dead of night,
   Lo, we saw a wondrous light;
   Angels singing peace on earth,
   Told us of the Saviour's birth."
           Hail, thou ever blessed . . .

5. Sacred Infant, all divine,
   What a tender love was Thine;
   Thus to come from highest bliss
   Down to such a world as this.
           Hail, thou ever blessed . . .

6. Teach, O teach us, Holy Child,
   By Thy face so meek and mild,
   Teach us to resemble Thee,
   In Thy sweet humility.
           Hail, thou ever blessed . . .

GOOD★KING★WENCESLAS

English Carol

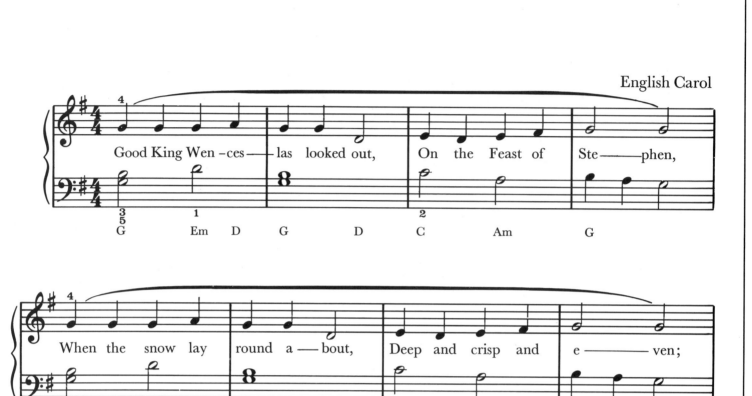

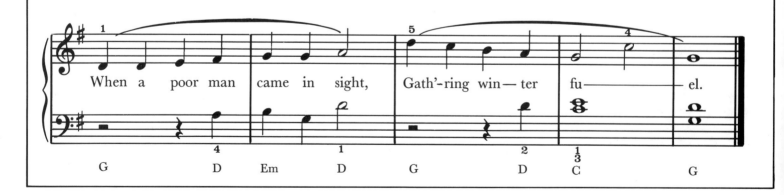

2. "Hither, page, and stand by me
   If thou know'st it, telling.
   Yonder peasant, who is he?
   Where and what his dwelling?"
"Sire, he lives a good league hence,
   Underneath the mountain,
   Right against the forest fence,
   By Saint Agnes' fountain."

3. "Bring me flesh, and bring me wine,
   Bring me pine logs hither;
   Thou and I will see him dine
   When we bear them thither."
Page and monarch forth they went,
   Forth they went together
Through the rude wind's wild lament
   And the bitter weather.

4. "Sire, the night is darker now,
   And the wind blows stronger;
   Fails my heart, I know not how,
   I can go no longer."
"Mark my footsteps, good my page,
   Tread thou in them boldly;
   Thou shalt find the winter's rage
   Freeze thy blood less coldly."

5. In his master's steps he trod,
   Where the snow lay dinted;
   Heat was in the very sod
   Which the saint had printed.
Therefore, Christian men, be sure,
   Wealth or rank possessing,
Ye who now will bless the poor
   Shall yourselves find blessing.

JUST ★ ANOTHER ★ STAR

Carol Barratt
Karl Jenkins

Just a-noth-er star to light the sky, Just a-noth-er town to pas-sers by, Just a-noth-er night so cold and grey, Stran-gers look for shelt-er, could-n't find a place to stay. Just a-noth-er donk—ey, warm and brown, Just a-noth-er jour—ney through the town,

2. Just another candle in the night,
   Just another shelter out of sight,
   Just another shepherd passin' by,
   Sheep stood round the manger listenin' to a lullaby.
   It was such a special place to stay,
   It was such a happy Christmas Day,
   It was such a glowing star that shone
   Up above the stable, where the Holy Child was born.
   Love isn't ever far . . .

ONCE★IN★ROYAL★DAVID'S★CITY

English Carol

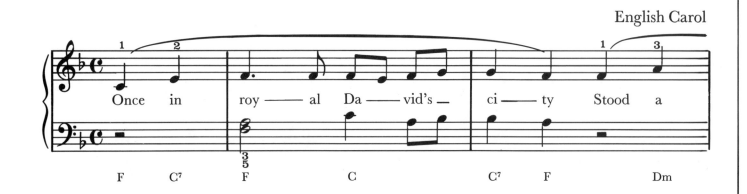

Once in roy — al Da — vid's ci — ty Stood a

F   C⁷   F   C   C⁷   F   Dm

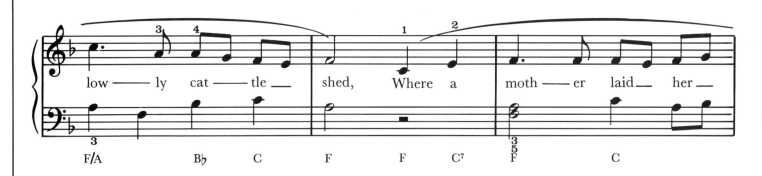

low — ly cat — tle shed, Where a moth — er laid her

F/A   B♭   C   F   F   C⁷   F   C

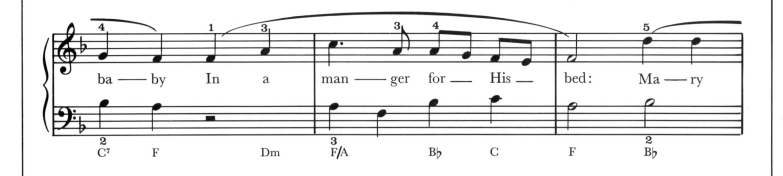

ba — by In a man — ger for His bed: Ma — ry

C⁷   F   Dm   F/A   B♭   C   F   B♭

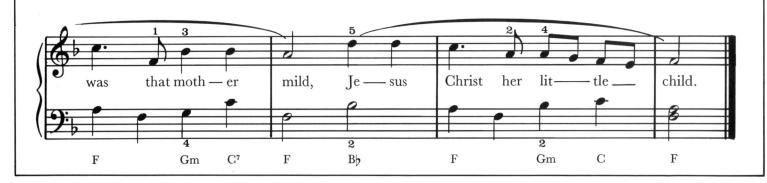

was that moth — er mild, Je — sus Christ her lit — tle child.

F   Gm   C⁷   F   B♭   F   Gm   C   F

2. He came down to earth from heaven
   Who is God and Lord of all,
   And His shelter was a stable,
   And His cradle was a stall;
   With the poor and mean and lowly
   Lived on earth our Saviour holy.

3. And through all His wondrous childhood
   He would honour and obey,
   Love and watch the lowly mother,
   In whose gentle arms He lay:
   Christian children all must be,
   Mild, obedient, good as He.

4. For He is our childhood's pattern,
   Day by day like us He grew;
   He was little, weak and helpless,
   Tears and smiles like us He knew.
   And He feeleth for our sadness,
   And He shareth in our gladness.

5. And our eyes at last shall see Him,
   Through His own redeeming love,
   For that child so dear and gentle
   Is our Lord in heaven above;
   And He leads His children on
   To the place where He is gone.

6. Not in that poor lowly stable,
   With the oxen standing by,
   We shall see Him; but in heaven,
   Set at God's right hand on high;
   Where like stars His children crowned
   All in white shall wait around.

JOLLY★OLD★SAINT★NICHOLAS

American Carol

2. When the clock is striking twelve,
   When I'm fast asleep,
   Down the chimney broad and black,
   With your pack you'll creep;
   All the stockings you will find
   Hanging in a row;
   Mine will be the shortest one,
   You'll be sure to know.

3. Johnny wants a pair of skates;
   Susy wants a sled;
   Nellie wants a picture book;
   Yellow, blue and red;
   Now I think I'll leave to you
   What to give the rest;
   Choose for me, dear Santa Claus,
   You will know the best.

O★COME★ALL★YE★FAITHFUL

English Carol

2. God of God,
   Light of light,
   Lo, He abhors not the Virgin's womb;
   Very God
   Begotten not created;
           O come, let us . . .

3. Sing, choirs of angels,
   Sing in exultation,
   Sing, all ye citizens of Heaven above,
   "Glory to God
   In the highest."
           O come, let us . . .

4. Yea, Lord, we greet Thee,
   Born this happy morning;
   Jesu, to Thee be glory given;
   Word of the Father,
   Now in flesh appearing;
           O come, let us . . .

O ★ LITTLE ★ TOWN ★ OF ★ BETHLEHEM

English Tune

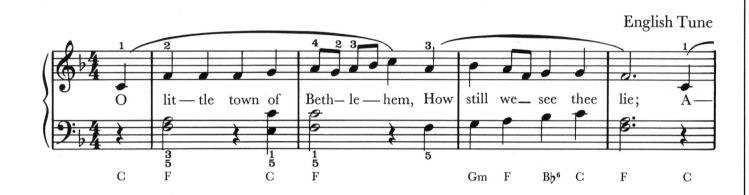

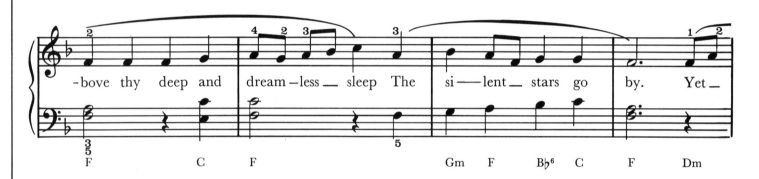

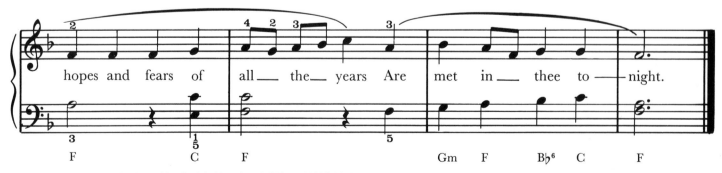

Melody collected and adapted by Ralph Vaughan Williams (1872-1958),
from the *English Hymnal* by permission of Oxford University Press.

2. How silently, how silently
   The wondrous gift is giv'n.
   So God imparts to human hearts
   The blessing of His heav'n.
   No ear may hear His coming;
   But in this world of sin,
   Where meek souls will receive Him, still
   The dear Christ enters in.

3. O Holy Child of Bethlehem
   Descend to us, we pray;
   Cast out our sin, and enter in,
   Be born in us today.
   We hear the Christmas angels
   The great glad tidings tell.
   O come to us, abide with us,
   Our Lord Emmanuel.

American Tune

DECK★THE★HALL

Welsh Carol

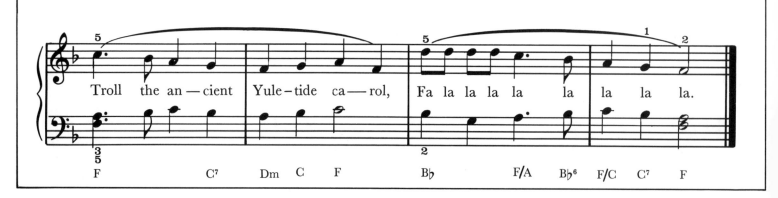

Deck the hall with boughs of hol—ly, Fa la la la la la la la la.

'Tis the sea—son to be jol—ly, Fa la la la la la la la la.

Don we now our gay ap—par—el, Fa la la la la la la la la.

Troll the an—cient Yule—tide ca—rol, Fa la la la la la la la la.

32

2. See the blazing Yule before us,
Fa la la la la la la la la.
Strike the harp and join the chorus,
Fa la la la la la la la la.
Follow me in merry measure,
Fa la la la la la la la la.
While I tell of Yuletide treasure,
Fa la la la la la la la la.

3. Fast away the old year passes,
Fa la la la la la la la la.
Hail the new, ye lads and lasses,
Fa la la la la la la la la.
Sing we joyous all together,
Fa la la la la la la la la.
Heedless of the wind and weather,
Fa la la la la la la la la.

ZITHER★CAROL

Words by Malcolm Sargent

Czech Folk Tune

Girls and boys, leave your toys, make no noise, Kneel at his crib and wor-ship Him. At thy shrine, Child di-vine, we are thine, Our Sa-viour's here. "Hal-le—lu——jah" the church bells ring, "Hal-le—lu——jah" the an——gels sing, "Hal-le—lu——jah" from ev'——ry——thing. All must draw near.

Words and simplified version of Malcolm Sargent's arrangement
by kind permission of Oxford University Press

2. On that day, far away, Jesus lay,
   Angels were watching round his head.
   Holy Child, Mother mild, undefiled,
   We sing thy praise.
   "Hallelujah" . . .
   Our hearts we raise.

3. Shepherds came, at the fame, of thy name,
   Angels their guide to Bethlehem.
   In that place, saw thy face, filled with grace,
   Stood at thy door.
   "Hallelujah" . . .
   Love evermore.

4. Wise men too, haste to do, homage new,
   Gold, myrrh and frankincense they bring.
   As 'twas said, starlight led, to thy bed,
   Bending their knee.
   "Hallelujah" . . .
   Worshipping thee.

5. Oh, that we, all might be, good as he,
   Spotless, with God in Unity.
   Saviour dear, ever near, with us here
   Since life began.
   "Hallelujah" . . .
   Godhead made man.

6. Cherubim, Seraphim, worship him,
   Sun, moon and stars proclaim his power.
   Everyday, on our way, we shall say
   Hallelujah.
   "Hallelujah" . . .
   Hallelujah.

SILENT★NIGHT

German Carol

36

2. Silent night, holy night:
   Shepherds quake at the sight;
   Glories stream from Heaven afar,
   Heavenly hosts sing Alleluia;
   Christ the Saviour is born,
   Christ the Saviour is born.

3. Silent night, holy night:
   Son of God, love's pure light;
   Radiant beams from Thy holy face,
   With the dawn of redeeming grace;
   Jesus, Lord, at Thy birth,
   Jesus, Lord, at Thy birth.

IT★CAME★UPON★THE★MIDNIGHT★CLEAR

English Tune

It___ came up—on the___ mid–night clear, That glo—rious song_ of

F   C   F   Gm   F   C   F   B♭

old, From_ An—gels bend–ing near the earth To___ touch their harps of

F   C   Dm   B♭   C   F   C⁷

gold. "Peace on the earth, good—will to men From heav'n's all—gra—cious

F   A   Dm   A⁷   Dm   C   Dm   C/G   G⁷

King." The world in sol—emn_ still–ness lay To___ hear_ the An—gels sing.

C   Am   Dm   Gm   F   C   F   F/C   C⁷   F

■ ■ ■ ■

American Tune

It came up —on___ the mid ——night clear, That

B♭   E♭   B♭   B♭

38

2. Still through the cloven skies they come   Above its sad and lowly plains
   With peaceful wings unfurled;   They bend on heavenly wing,
   And still their heavenly music floats   And ever o'er its Babel sounds
   O'er all the weary world;   The blessèd Angels sing.

WE★WISH★YOU★A★MERRY★CHRISTMAS

English Carol

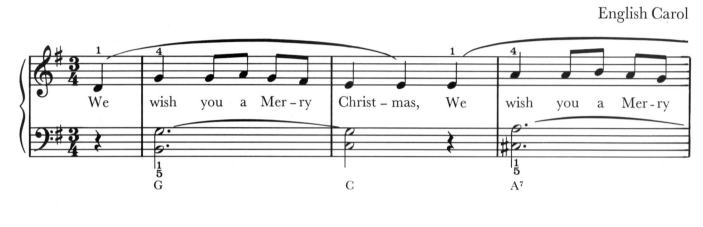

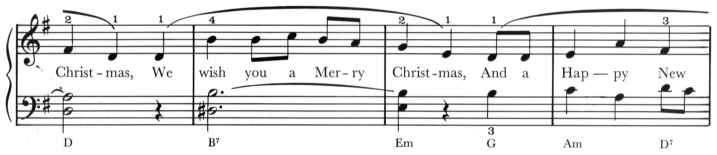

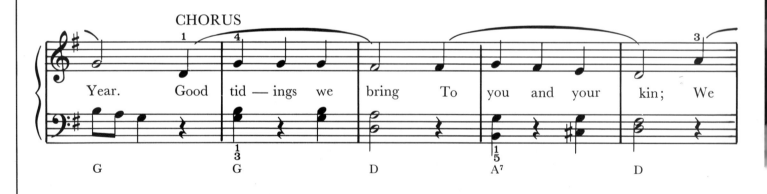

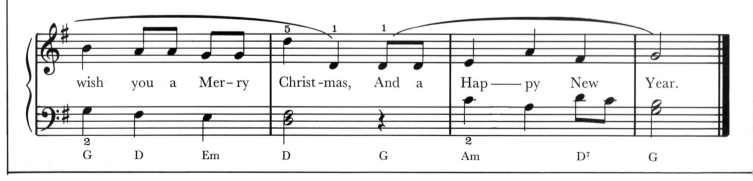

8/01 (41185)

Reproduced and printed b
Halstan & Co. Ltd., Amersham, Bucks., Englan